MADAGASCAR

For Scott,
who, four years ahead
of me at NCSA, showed me
what an actor was. For this
and your friendship, I will
always be grateful.
Your true friend,

Mary Beth Peil as Lilian, Sherri Parker Lee as June, and Larry Pine as Nathan in the Adirondack Theatre Festival production of *Madagascar*.

MADAGASCAR

A PLAY BY

J. T. Rogers

FOREWORD BY FRANCIS GILLEN

 University of Tampa Press • Tampa, Florida

On the cover: Detail from Giovanni Lorenzo Bernini's sculpture "Pluto and Persephone" (1622). Photograph by Steve Decker.

Photographs from the SPF New York City production copyright © 2005 by Carol Rosegg. The original marble fragment from the Eleusinian Relief, ca. 440-430 B.C., is in the National Museum, Athens; a Roman copy is in the collection of the Metropolitan Museum of Art.

Manufactured in the United States of America
Book design by Richard Mathews
Printed on acid-free paper ∞
First Edition

University of Tampa Press
401 West Kennedy Blvd.
Tampa, FL 33606

ISBN 1-879852-43-3 (cloth)
ISBN 1-879852--44-0 (pbk.)

Browse & order online at
http://utpress.ut.edu

Library of Congress Cataloging-in-Publication Data

Rogers, J. T., 1968-
  Madagascar : a play / by J. T. Rogers.-- 1st ed.
    p. cm.
  ISBN-13: 978-1-879852-43-3 (cloth : acid-free paper)
  ISBN-10: 1-879852-43-8 (cloth : acid-free paper)
  ISBN-13: 978-1-879852-44-0 (pbk. : acid-free paper)
  ISBN-10: 1-879852-44-6 (pbk. : acid-free paper)
  1. Tour guides (Persons)--Drama. 2. Mothers and daughters--Drama. 3. Americans--Italy--Drama. 4. College teachers--Drama. 5. Missing persons--Drama. 6. Rome (Italy)--Drama. 7. Hotels--Drama. I. Title.
  PS3618.O463M33 2005
  812'.6--dc22   2005019800

For my family

Acknowledgments

When Nancy Borgenicht and Allen Nevins of the Salt Lake Acting Company commissioned *Madagascar,* they told me: "We believe in you; write whatever you want and we'll stage it." And they did. For such extraordinary faith and support, I thank them and everyone at SLAC.

Much of this play was written while in residence at the Edward Albee Foundation, and then honed while in residence at the Eugene O'Neill Theater Center, where I was sponsored by Epic Repertory Theatre. I am indebted to all three organizations.

I am blessed to have readers whose comments and criticisms continue to push me to become a better writer. *Madagascar* was greatly improved by the suggestions of Mike Dorrell, David Mong, David Rogers, Lauren Sanders, and Susan Spencer Smith. I am, as always, in their debt.

I am indebted as well to John Buzzetti and Sherri Parker Lee—tireless advocates for and passionate champions of my work. I thank them both.

Years of conversations with Dr. Eric Helland, professor of economics at Claremont McKenna College, helped shape this play. For his expertise and friendship, I am grateful.

Finally, and most importantly, I wish to thank Rebecca Ashley and Gus Reyes—one, my wife; one, my director; both, my dearest friends and confidants. Without their suggestions, support, and stewardship, this play, like so much of my work, would not exist. They have my love and my gratitude.

Anne Cullimore Decker as Lilian in the Salt Lake Acting Company production of *Madagascar*. Photo by Scott Peterson.

Foreword

In his play *Madagascar* J.T. Rogers gives us a hauntingly poetic evocation of our human need for knowledge of ourselves and others, and the consequences of our failure to obtain it. Its characters are born or ascend to privilege; its images are often those of claustrophobia: vestal virgins entombed, a set that opens with light and view, and closes with the same room evoking a prison. These characters, like us, are prisoners of themselves, of what habit and character cause them to see and fail to see. In Rogers' intense vision, Madagascar becomes everything about ourselves and others that is just out of reach, a fingertip beyond, eluding somehow our words and perceptions. What we know about ourselves finally, if we do achieve some self-knowledge, is that those fingers we reach toward "other" are crushed, or amputated, and that we ourselves may have done the cutting. Or maybe, in an existential sense, they were never there.

Setting the play in an expensive hotel room in Rome, looking down on the Spanish steps, provides its sense of history. The characters act out their drama against a background that evokes the universality of their very particular and nuanced situation. The catalyst of much of the action is significantly the one character who is never present on stage except in the memories of the others, the absent son, twin brother, accuser. The dramatic spine of *Madagascar* is absence. This is what the three characters must confront and sort out. Their responsibility. What they missed.

I believe the play is also political in the deepest sense, not in rehearsing political slogans or agendas, but in examining the human roots of our political failure, the self-absorption that keeps us from perceiving "other." The rooms which, Pinter-like, built out of our needs and fears, become the prisons of our limited perceptions. And outside our privileged room? The Aids crisis in Africa. The 30,000 children who die each day of poverty-related hunger or disease. Civilian casualties.

But it is the power of Rogers' language, together with his vision, that makes him a unique new voice in theatre. As image and motif echo one another—the fingers, the elusive fish of childhood experience, the statues of antiquity, the room, the title—we know the ritual that is the play *Madagascar* will haunt us long after we have exited the theatre. For like Greek tragedy, *Madagascar* is a ritual acknowledgment of a world in which we need to walk warily, humanly, humbly, precisely because there is so much we do not, maybe cannot, know.

Francis Gillen
Editor, *The Pinter Review*

MADAGASCAR

Brenda Sue Cowley as June, Joe Cronin as Nathan, and Anne Cullimore Decker as Lilian in the Salt Lake Acting Company production of *Madagascar*. Photo by Scott Peterson.

Larry Pine as Nathan, Mary Beth Peil as Lilian, and Sherri Parker Lee as June in the Off-Broadway SPF Summer Play Festival production of *Madagascar*.

Production History

Madagascar was commissioned and given its world premier by the Salt Lake Acting Company (Nancy Borgenicht and Allen Nevins, executive producers; David Kirk Chambers, managing director) on November 16, 2004. The artists involved were as follows:

June	Brenda Sue Cowley
Lilian	Anne Cullimore Decker
Nathan	Joe Cronin
Director	Gus Reyes
Set designer	Keven Myhre
Lighting designer	James M. Craig
Sound designer	Cynthia L. Kehr
Costume designer	Brenda Van der Weil
Stage manager	Tanner Broughton

Madagascar was then presented in New York as a coproduction of the SPF Summer Play Festival (Arielle Tepper, founder and executive producer; Rachel Neuburger, artistic director) and the Adirondack Theatre Festival (Martha Banta, artistic director; David Turner, producing director). The play opened Off Broadway on July 12, 2005, and then again at the Adirondack Theatre Festival on July 20, 2005. The artists involved were as follows:

June	Sherri Parker Lee
Lilian	Mary Beth Peil
Nathan	Larry Pine
Director	Gus Reyes
Producer	Dean Strober
Set designer	Eric Renschler
Lighting designer	Les Dickert
Sound designer	Darron L West
Costume designer	Susan J. Slack
Stage manager	Jennifer Rogers

Mary Beth Peil as Lilian, Sherri Parker Lee as June, and Larry Pine as Nathan in the Off-Broadway SPF Summer Play Festival production of *Madagascar*. Photo by Carol Rosegg.

Characters

June
A woman in her early thirties
Also plays FEMALE PASSENGER *and* WOMAN

Lilian
A woman around sixty
Also plays FEMALE TOURIST *and* FEMALE TOURIST TWO,
THREE, *and* FOUR; FEMALE RELIEF WORKER; EMBASSY WOMAN;
and FUNERAL GUEST

Nathan
A man around sixty
Also plays MALE TOURIST, *and* MALE TOURIST TWO *and* THREE;
ECONOMIST; MAN; MALE RELIEF WORKER; *and* FELLOW TRAVELER

Place

Rome. *A hotel room above the Piazza di Spagna, looking down on the Spanish Steps.*

Time

Three different periods: LILIAN, *five years ago;* JUNE, *a few days ago;* NATHAN, *the present.*

PROLOGUE

Brenda Sue Cowley as June in the Salt Lake Acting Company's production of *Madagascar*. Photo by Scott Peterson.

PROLOGUE

In the darkness we hear a movement from Bach's "Six Suites for Unaccompanied Cello." In the slowly rising light we begin to make out the projected image of a fragment of the Eleusinian Relief: two women and a boy between them, all carved in marble. The movement ends as the image comes sharply into focus.

A shaft of light reveals JUNE, *center stage. She is in her early thirties, barefoot, dressed in a simple white linen nightgown. Surrounded by darkness, she speaks directly to us.*

JUNE

People disappear all the time. I don't mean children who are taken or stolen and then, so often . . . well, we all know enough about that. I mean *people*, the over-eighteen kind. Thousands and thousands, every year. Almost all of them end up being found. Very few are murdered. Comfortingly few. Statistically, fewer than two percent are victims of "foul play." Which always makes me think of exuberant chickens running around.

(*Beat.*) Or maybe that's just me.

Those who aren't found, nine times out of ten it's because they chose to go missing. (*Beat.*) I didn't know this. That so many people choose to step away from their lives. They owe money, someone's pregnant, they've done a terrible thing, or they've just had enough. Life rises and rises, until all you can do is drown or swim away. And if you haven't broken any laws, this is perfectly legal. Even if you were tracked down, say, paddling the Congo or wandering alone in the Sahara, no one can force you to go back. If you choose to vanish, you owe your past nothing.

[3]

But what interests me most are those left behind. The ones forced to go on, never knowing if they said or did something that led to the vanishing. If they are honest, they will tell you that even when all evidence points to a planned disappearance . . . they will themselves to reject this, and cling to any alternative they can find . . . even death.

They will tell you that if someone is going to choose to disappear, they need to stay gone. That what is feared most is a return. Because some do. The tiniest percentage, but they do. Even after years, they just . . . reappear. As vengefully as they disappeared.

Some things cannot be faced.

(A stream of light reveals LILIAN, *sitting stage right. She is around sixty, elegantly dressed in pants and a sweater. She sits in a chair, legs crossed. There are pearls at her throat. She smiles as she speaks to us.)*

LILIAN

When I fly, wherever I fly, I am always asked, even at my age: "And what do *you* do?" Every flight, every time. New York to Geneva, Geneva to Rome—

"And what do *you* do?"

I understand this is self-protection. We live in dangerous times. Buckling in, people are desperate for conversation. Anything that will divert them from the slim but real possibility that our time together will end in a screaming, fiery death. And who wants to sip a wine spritzer and talk about that. But I have always found the question deeply unnerving. Every time I am asked—still—my mouth goes dry and my mind goes blank. If I were honest, I would simply lean in and say:

(She does so, speaking intimately to her seatmate . . .) "I stay in motion."

But who wouldn't prefer a screaming, fiery death over talking to someone like that?

I am not trying to be coy. I *know* this is not the most thunderously impressive achievement to hang a life on. But it is what defines me. We are who we are: there is no escape from that. And, of course, I regret this lack of achievement. I find, more and more, I regret a great deal. There are days when I swim in an ocean of regret. Not that I burden others with this. Certainly not my children. After all, there is nothing more tedious than your own parents' disappointment. And now I have *no* idea where I was going with all this—totally lost; full stop; another wine spritzer, please.

(A realization; she smiles.)

But this has now become a perfect example of why one stays in motion. Because what I have learned in life is that no matter what happens, no matter how lost you are, you must always keep going forward. This is the first of my three golden rules. For if one simply talks and talks, things, often for the first time, become clear. When one is faced with the unfathomable, all one can do is speak through it. This is the only hope you have of untangling a mystery.

(We hear footsteps, as NATHAN *walks out of the darkness and toward us from stage left. He is around sixty, in slacks and a sports coat. His clothes are rumpled, his face unshaven, and his eyes bleary. He stops at mid-stage and speaks to us.)*

NATHAN

I enter the room, I see five men. This is the only part I ever remember. The walls are white. Naked lightbulb. A man sits in a chair in front of a table. He's dressed in black, head to toe, with a thick mane of black hair. Three heavies, they're holding his hands down, pinning him so he can't get up. The last fellow stands to the side, asking questions. Question after question. And the man in the chair won't answer, so they start cutting his fingers off with a saw. The palms are held down, and the saw cuts into the bone—

(He holds up his hands, the backs of them facing us.)

Here, right above the knuckles. The blood gushes everywhere, across the table, onto the floor. The man in black is screaming; both hands are cut halfway through. A few more sawings and his fingers will be totally severed. But I force myself not to look away. Grit my teeth so I don't vomit. Because my job is to collect information. I have to watch this. That's why I'm here. The man is *screaming,* like a wounded animal, snot runs out of his nose, eyes roll back in his head . . . I'm the man. The one being maimed. The shock of this realization is what wakes me. And what I'm left with, every time, is guilt. A vice on my chest, squeezing me. Because I'm a traitor; I've torn everything down.

Now I have to be punished.

ACT ONE

Mary Beth Peil as Lilian and Larry Pine as Nathan in the Off-Broadway SPF Summer Play Festival production of *Madagascar*. Photo by Carol Rosegg.

ACT ONE

A shift of light. Music.

For a moment, the three of them are in tableau: their bodies frozen against the image of the two women and the boy, carved in stone.

A shift of light again, brighter now, as the image changes. Behind them, we see a projection of the Spanish Steps in the Piazza di Spagna, Rome.

On the stage we see a once grand hotel room now stripped of its finery: a simple bed and nightstand, a chair and table, a window frame. Where a chandelier used to hang, there is only a dangling lightbulb. Throughout, everyone is on stage—in this room, but at their own specific point in time.

NATHAN *and* LILIAN *begin to walk toward the lip of the stage as* JUNE *speaks to us.*

Behind her, we see briefly the faint outline of the words: A FEW DAYS AGO.

JUNE

Most of the groups I show around Rome are American. I only do small groups, a dozen people at most. Bigger than that, you have to use microphones and wear name tags. Spending my days wearing a sticker over my breast that says "June" is . . . well, when I moved here from New York three years ago, it was to get away from things like that. The anonymity of this work is what makes it so appealing. I don't know you; you don't know me: we can be anyone we want.

(NATHAN and LILIAN have reached the edge of the stage. Throughout, all three actors play the secondary characters that appear. Throughout, as they move to and fro about the room—sitting in a chair, looking out the window, crossing to the veranda; even when physically touching and looking at each other—everything is addressed to us.)

FEMALE TOURIST

(Brightly.) We're from Boulder!

MALE TOURIST

Santa Monica!

JUNE

I always ask where they're from.

FEMALE TOURIST TWO

Iowa City.

JUNE

People like that.

FEMALE TOURIST TWO

That's in Iowa.

LILIAN

They come from all over: St. Louis, Atlanta, but in every group, I mean *every* group, there's at least one person from . . .

(It is as if she is surrounded by a group of Morristownians firing away at her.)

MALE TOURIST TWO

Morristown.

FEMALE TOURIST THREE

I live in Morristown.

MALE TOURIST THREE & FEMALE TOURIST FOUR

(Together.)

We're from Morristown, New Jersey!

LILIAN

I find this more than strange. I mean, the number of people I've taken through the Forum that are from— It's just one town. Statistically, this makes no sense. But every time I start my tour right down the street from my room here, at the top of the Spanish Steps, pointing out Keats's house— *(As if to them.)* There, on your left, ladies and gentleman— Before they can say *anything,* hairs go up on the back of my neck, and I know: Morristown is among us.

My father always said there's no such thing as a coincidence. "Dig deeper," he'd say. "Find the connection," he'd say. "That's how you unlock a mystery."

Today, in the Coliseum, while they were running around snapping their digital photos instead of just standing still and experiencing the awe that comes from being in such a place . . . I watched them. Trying to find some, some *clue* that would—an *answer* to—

What does this mean? What am I missing?

Then I heard Paul, his lips pressed next to my ear:

"You're not paying attention," he says. "It's when you're not paying attention that you miss things."

(LILIAN *turns to us. We are, as always, in the same hotel room, but now, for a moment, we see the ghostly projection of the words:* FIVE YEARS AGO.)

LILIAN

I'd forgotten how crowded this city is. Years since I've been here. I used to come like clockwork, by myself or with my children, Gideon and June. We always stayed in this hotel just off the Piazza di Spagna, here in my favorite room. I take great comfort in routine. And how could one *not* be comforted, surrounded by chandeliers and furniture of such elegance and craftsmanship.

I'd take them by the hand and we'd stand out on that veranda.

(She points out in front of us.)

"Just look," I'd tell them. "Can you feel the layers of history. The secrets."

Arthur never cared for this city. No interest in it whatsoever. Every year, I would entreat him to join me:

(As if to him.) "Rome is our mirror, dear, giving us a sense of who we are in its reflection. Caesar! Virgil! *(Alluringly.)* Sacrificial virgins!"

I tried everything. But antiquity did not hold my husband in her grip. For Arthur, what fascinated was "The Dark Continent." Ghana, Madagascar—*Always* Madagascar. The *time* he spent working there.

My husband was an economist. A very good one, I'm told. Certainly in demand. Governments, universities—a whirl of motion. I have no idea *what* he did, but he seemed to do it very well. This was hardly my fault, as Arthur worked in a field inhospitable to those who don't speak the language. Economists, at least from the point of view of someone married into the profession, seem only to be able to speak in paragraphs. With footnotes. You must be very careful when you ask them a question. Even the most innocent, even the most isn't-the-weather-nice-and-didn't-you-like-the-wine question can lead to an oration of mind-numbing length. More than once I've asked someone to pass the salmon, only to be given a lecture on diminishing marginal utility. But what's *most* galling is the constant assumption that you are interested. One of his colleagues prefaces all his pontifications with:

ECONOMIST

This you'll find interesting.

LILIAN

Every time. Just launches in.

ECONOMIST

This you'll find interesting.

LILIAN

No rhyme, no reason.

ECONOMIST

This you'll find—

LILIAN

(As if to the man.) How would you know, *since you won't stop talking? (Suddenly enraged.)* You do not *know* me! YOU WILL NEVER KNOW ME!

(Pause, as she collects herself.)

Arthur was much too tasteful for that sort of thing. In mixed company, he kept his equations to himself. He *was* charming. Utterly. Handsome, witty—and the way he dressed! But most of all it was his hair . . . that beautiful, thick black mane he always ran his fingers through. This is what women found so . . . Not that he dallied. As I said, Arthur's mistress was his work. Madagascar: all consuming, always taking him from us. We never spoke of this. Before his death. We never spoke of many things. But if we are honest, we must admit that the longer you know someone—*truly* know them—the less you can say. Over time, your tongue becomes frozen like a statue, and the words, the ones you *need* . . . lie just out of reach.

(As NATHAN *crosses to us, we fleetingly see the words:* THE PRESENT.*)*

NATHAN

On the flight over here last night, and this you'll find interesting, I had one of those . . . I'm not sure how you describe it, but "spooky" is the word that comes to mind. Spooky but comforting, if you can imagine it. We hadn't even left the States, still on the tarmac, getting buckled in—

FEMALE PASSENGER

So what do *you* do?

NATHAN

Woman next to me, just trying to make conversation. *(As if to his fellow passenger.)* I'm an economic theorist.

FEMALE PASSENGER

Really. Is that, like, interest rates? Inflation?

NATHAN

No, no. That's macro. I do micro. They look at the forests, we look at the trees. Strictly a tree man.

FEMALE PASSENGER

. . . Hunh.

NATHAN

You see, the bedrock principle of microtheory is that when you start with competitive exchange between individuals with well-defined preference orderings, you can prove there exists a Pareto efficient . . .

(The FEMALE PASSENGER *begins to snore. After a beat,* NATHAN *turns back to us.)*

Happens every time. I don't have the ability to articulate the—to find the *words* when I need them most. I freeze up, I just—

(As if to her, with gravitas.) Whatever people do, they have a very good reason to do so. What is done—*whatever* action is done—is for a reason. Woven together, these actions create a pattern. As a microtheorist, it's my job to figure out what that pattern means.

FEMALE PASSENGER

(Sexily.) Wow.

(They stare longingly at each other . . . until he turns from his "fantasy" and speaks to us.)

NATHAN

Why the hell couldn't I have just said that! I'm playing this over in my head the rest of the flight, taxi to the hotel, checking in—*People do things.* Mathematical models, utility functions: these are just tools to get to the hidden answers underneath. Look at the wide world. People do things here on God's green earth that, on the surface, make no sense. You pay four dollars for a cup of coffee, you vote for Democrats, you take a bottle of sleeping pills. Why do you do this? *(Pause.)* I need to know why you do this.

And sitting on that plane, from the moment I opened my mouth and started failing, once again, to explain all this . . . I could feel him. As if Arthur was still alive, sitting next to me. His voice in my ear, saying what he always said:

"You're not seeing the pattern, Nathan. Don't let the details of reality blind you to the truth."

LILIAN

When my visit here is over, I fly straight back to my lake house in Switzerland. Town outside Geneva where I spend two months every summer, like clockwork. Tiny lake, mountain air, shingled cottage: poetry. Ever since Arthur's death, I . . . To *know* there is a cottage, nestled in the mountains, waiting for me. That I shall be able to swim alone in that lake, shedding my cares stroke by stroke. The security of that gives me such comfort. This is what I have always told my son:

(As if to him.) "Without comfort, dear, what hope do you have for happiness? My darling, we must be safe to be happy. We are *here* to be happy."

My son's plane arrives this morning . . . *(checks her watch)* at any moment. In his letter, in that small, precise script of his, he was very clear about what time we should meet here. My son has *always* written me. Letters, postcards, clippings about things that dovetail with my interests. Always with notes from him in the margins. Elliptical riddles for me to unwind. This has been our little game—just we two—for years.

Today I've reserved him his own room. After all, he's not a boy anymore. And we both have *very* clear ideas about how one arranges toiletries. One of the things I did not foresee about being so rigidly opinionated is what happens when you pass this trait on.

My son is my favorite. I know we're not supposed to have favorites, but all parents do. Whatever we tell others, or ourselves, we *all* do. And when I see the passion he has for . . . *(She sweeps her arm out toward us.)* all of this. To have worked so hard, and to see that spark catch. Just thinking about it gives me goose bumps. Every time. Gideon. *(Slowly savoring the words.)* Gideon Doyle. *(Then, distastefully.)* Gideon *Paul* Doyle. The Paul part still irritates me. "Paul," as in "small," as in, not any child of mine. But *all* the men in Arthur's family have that as their middle name. Some things, you discover in life, cannot be changed. Gideon was my choice. I wanted something Old Testament-like, almost musty. Ahab was in the running for a while, but the whaling motif sunk it in the end. Something permanent. That's what I was after. Implacable as stone. I can't remember how or where it came to me, but when I looked it up, "Gideon," it said. "Feller of trees." And I thought:

"Yes, he will. Clear forests, empty fields. And I shall be so proud."

JUNE

I thought about Paul all through today's tour. Especially when we ended at the Temple of Vesta.

MALE TOURIST

(A little too eager.) So where are the virgins?

JUNE

Everyone wants to see it. They've all heard the stories.

MALE TOURIST

Are those them? The statues?

JUNE

The temple had a flame that burned through the centuries until the sack of Rome.

MALE TOURIST

(Staring intently at them.) Where are their heads?

JUNE

It burned in honor of the goddess Vesta, and was tended by the Vestal Virgins.

MALE TOURIST

(As if talking to his companion.) Why the heck don't they have heads?

FEMALE TOURIST

(Exasperated.) Would you let her talk!

JUNE

There's always some older woman fascinated by this next part.

FEMALE TOURIST

You never let people talk!

MALE TOURIST

Virgins should have heads: that's all I'm saying!

JUNE

It's uncanny how much she always reminds me of my mother.

FEMALE TOURIST

(To June.) You were saying?

JUNE

But ever since I moved here three years ago, every woman over a certain age reminds me of Lily.

FEMALE TOURIST

Go on, dear.

JUNE

(As if she is speaking to her tour.) To be a vestal was the greatest honor a woman could attain. They were selected when they were little girls, their lives dedicated to this one sacred task. They were glorified. Just their touch would spare a condemned man from death. The key, of course, was keeping up the virgin part. If you didn't, you were killed in a very interesting way.

FEMALE & MALE TOURIST

(Together.) Really!

JUNE

(Back to us.) Everyone's with me at this point. Virgins and death are always a winning combination. The girl was led through the streets, which were lined with people, silently staring. The only sound was the wheels of the horse-drawn cart on the cobblestones. She was wound through the city, out the gates, taken to a cave, given a loaf of soda bread and a lit candle. Then she was sealed inside. When the bread was eaten, she had a choice: keep the darkness at bay but have the oxygen quickly burn away or sit longer in the blackness and contemplate her crime.

FEMALE AND MALE TOURIST

(Together. Quietly.) . . . That poor girl.

JUNE

Today, after we shook hands and they all started to drift off, I . . .
It was like I became rooted in front of the statues.

FEMALE TOURIST

How frightened she must have been.

JUNE

What did they do? That's what Paul and I always asked
each other. Every time we stood in front of them. Did they
claw their hands against the stones, until their fingers . . . or
did they, alone in the dark . . . did they welcome it. Because
if they were honest . . . part of them must have wanted to be
punished.

MALE TOURIST

(*Very gently.*) Someone should have helped her.

JUNE

To be absolved of their crime.

FEMALE TOURIST

Someone should have tried.

JUNE

Purification. Then release.

NATHAN

In my line of work, it's the hidden connections *between* actions that fascinate. "We traffic in secrets," Arthur would say. "Untangling mysteries. Step by step." For example, one moment you can be sitting at your desk editing a speech, preparing for the most important conference of your career. The phone rings, and, suddenly, you rush to the airport, board a plane, and then you find yourself on the other side of the world in an empty hotel room. . . .

(He looks around the room.)

Doing nothing. People have spent entire careers trying to uncover the connections to something like that.

I'd forgotten that this city is so convoluted. Walking over here this morning, I got totally lost. And my hotel's just a few blocks from the Spanish Steps, for God's sake. How do people *live* here? It makes you realize, a grid is a beautiful thing.

I know, no matter how many times you come here, you're supposed to be moved. Strolling through the Forum, the Coliseum: Oh, the antiquity! Oh, the humanity! Woo-hoo! Yes, well, there was a time when I found this city . . . *(Searching for the right words.)* magnificent. This room . . . it looked so different back then . . . it was the most important place in the world to me.

(He points out over our heads.)

But being here again, today, after so many years . . . standing out on that balcony: all I see is ruins. Then again, I never came here for the architecture.

(Again, he slowly looks around.)

I never wanted to come here again.

LILIAN

I had been so looking forward to the quiet of these cobbled streets. Gideon and I used to go shopping, down there, in the boutiques around the Spanish Steps. For a mother to have a son who likes to go shopping is as close to heaven as most of us get. Even among the young and elegant all around us, he was head-turningly beautiful. Gray flannel trousers and a blue blazer, everywhere. Very Brooks Brothers. Very fifteen going on forty, and where's my pipe. *(Remembering.)* No! Not *even* fifteen. Still with peach fuzz. Young enough to let me touch him and run my fingers through his hair.

But it appears that in my long absence from here, the Visigoths have descended. Now on the Steps, all the young people are sandaled and unwashed and look like they desperately need a good meal. I find this mystifying. These are the children of wealth and privilege. Who else but the wealthy and privileged can afford to fly here? Yet here they are, trying desperately to pretend they are "the other." This, this *obsession* now in the young to—where does it come from?—that you must suffer. That denial and deprivation are what give life meaning.

"If only I were diseased! If only I were starving! If only I were a famine victim with a hacked off limb! Then I'd really *be* someone!"

How destructive! Foolish! We are here for comfort! Happiness! We—

"That's not true, Mother."

Gideon would say this, whenever I rose up on my high horse. Even as a boy.

"We are here for other things."

(As if to him.) "Like what, dear?" *(To us.)* I would test him. Try and get him to learn how to articulate his point. *(To him.)* "Then exactly what are we here for?"

" . . . Like . . .

"Yes?"

"Like . . . "

"Go on."

" . . . Like . . . "

"*Tell me.*"

(To us.) Of course he never could. I mean, at that age—but how he'd try. Furrow-browed, chopping the air with his hands. In those moments—it was there, flashing in his eyes—his most fervent wish: to prove me wrong. Pull me down from my pedestal. Every bone in his little body, wanting it so badly.

But then, you see, I remember—so clearly—I would kiss his head, and we would go to the Trevi Fountain; eat gelato, throw coins, and we *were*. Happy.

JUNE

Before each tour I have coffee and read the paper here in my room. Someone leaves them outside my door with the mail, on those rare occasions when I have mail. Coffee, paper, tour: I do the same thing every day. The structure gives me something to sink my teeth into. It's important in life to always have something in front of you that you can focus on and move toward. "Look at your feet," that's one of my rules. "Go forward, keep your eyes in front of you, and *don't . . . look . . . back.*" That's the key. Because when you do . . . for me . . . it's like there's a mountain. Looming. And I stand like a statue, frozen in the shadow of it.

(She points to a man's blue work shirt, faded and well-worn, and a pair of trousers.)

I wear the same thing here, every day. Wash it out in the sink, let it dry in the sun. Living here, on my own, it's been amazing to discover what you can do without.

(She gestures to the room around her.)

If you strip away the things that surround you, you learn what you truly need.

This room. It's embarrassing how much it costs. (Not that you can tell, since my "renovation.") Yes, the view from the balcony is lovely; but for the price of living in a hotel these past three years, I could have bought an entire villa. But this was our room. And as my father used to say, "That which we most want, we do. Regardless."

Money isn't an issue for me, of course. Paul would always remind me of that. How lucky we were. Spoiled. Paul wouldn't have to *say* this. Just a look, and I'd know. Because we knew each other. Down to our bones. Right now, Paul could be sitting in a room— anywhere in the world—he'd know what I was going to say or do next. And why. Everyone needs someone like that. A mirror you can see your reflection in. Making life worth living.

(Beat.)

But living here, I've also discovered the *danger* in learning new things. Because if you keep digging, one day you'll discover that something you know in your bones, that defines who you are . . . is a lie.

NATHAN

My red-eye back to the States leaves at nine. If I stay awake on the flight, I'll still have enough time to finish preparing. I'm delivering a paper tomorrow on—well, *the* paper, actually. Primo time slot, packed room, quite a coup . . . No, *more* than that. It's a once-in-a-lifetime opportunity. A second chance to get my hat in the ring. This late in the game, that's a rare thing.

The conference is about the work Arthur was doing before his
. . . "passing" has a nice, bloodless ring to it, doesn't it? Let's go
with "passing." All I'm doing—for years now—is standing on his
shoulders. It's Arthur's flag; I'm just waving it. He was doing some
remarkable work. Even now, after all these years, you have to ask,
What if? How far would he have gone?

Arthur had this relentless focus. The ability to slice to the core of
a question. Even when we were in graduate school it was obvious.
The response when he published that first article. My contributions
to the field have been a bit more unimpactful. In the hard sciences,
you have a limited window. When you're young is when you have
to make your mark. Contribute something of your *own*, before the
mind fogs over and you become just another tweed-coat, knit-tie
member of the establishment.

But with Arthur, it wasn't just his mind. He had . . . *it*. When
he'd open his mouth, people would listen. It was as simple as that.
Students, congressmen, World Bank officials. I'd watch him draw
them in with that distracted way of his, never quite looking you in
the eye, his hands chopping the air. It was like they were painting
a picture while he talked. He's speaking—you can *see* them going
up on their toes, leaning in, trying to . . . and he would rock back
on his heels, just out of reach.

Arthur's work was his life. It was cruel the way he shut people
out. Even his children. A great man or a great father: you don't get
to be one without giving up the other.

LILIAN

I have not *seen* my son in six months. This is his first trip back
from Africa. The excitement has made me sleepless for days. A brief
rendezvous is all this is. Gideon has already spent the bulk of his

furlough visiting June back home in New York. This is just a stopover before he returns to his work. All we'll have time for are a couple of personal highlights, then back on our respective planes. We'll start with the Forum, after he's unpacked and arranged his toiletries. I *always* took them to the Forum. Even at home our weekly outing was a day at the Greco-Roman wing at the Metropolitan. Sunday mornings: some people take their children to church, I took mine to the museum. The Greek statues were what captivated us. Those marble, life-sized Greek figures of the men and women of antiquity. We would stroll among them, hand in hand, as they towered over us, frozen in time. And to think that these exact figures stood, twenty-five hundred years ago, gazing out on the Aegean, and that they are with us still. Goose bumps, every time.

And the Museo Borghese! How I've *dreamed* these last few weeks of the Borghese! This will *have* to be the other sight Gideon and I see. It holds Bernini's "Pluto and Persephone," the most exquisite statue I have ever seen. The goddess Persephone caught in the arms of Pluto, lord of the netherworld. There in stone, he grips her as she calls out, kicking and screaming. And the details—It must be *seen*! I cannot do it justice!—It is his hand that always draws me. Every muscle, throbbing with desire. I have always felt what is so haunting is that she is on the cusp of surrender. Of giving over to his ravishing, and being dragged down into darkness. I find the idea of that . . . immensely appealing. Because I, too, wish to be punished. I don't mean velvet handcuffs and a riding crop. We've all done a bit of that. Haven't we. Something violent. Shameful. Because, like everyone, I have done selfish, terrible things. And sins must be paid for. If we are ever to be purified. Then released.

NATHAN

Being around Arthur could be a bit overwhelming. I don't just mean the work. Socializing with—well, his whole family. "The

House of Doyle." People like that, for someone like me . . . Let's just say, the first time I went to dinner at their apartment, there were eating utensils around my plate I'd never seen. And you sit there, at that long oaken table, with the chandeliers and the bone china and the privilege just reeking off everything, and you can't not be envious. If you're honest.

LILIAN

(As if greeting a guest.) Thank you so much for coming!

NATHAN

God! The parties were the worst!

LILIAN

You look ravishing as ever, dear!

NATHAN

I'd be so nervous, I'd start babbling in jargon.

LILIAN

I'm so sorry Arthur couldn't be here!

NATHAN

As if English were a foreign language.

LILIAN

Blame the government, blame Africa, just don't blame me!

NATHAN

I'd stand over the punch bowl and hear myself saying:

(Chuckling to someone, as he tries to be suave.) "Well, a few more glasses of this and we'll have an example of the law of diminishing marginal utility." *(He laughs; no one else does. Back to us.)* Women do not find this attractive.

LILIAN

(Seeing him for the first time.) Nathan!

NATHAN

Then one night—This was over twenty years ago, you understand. But some things you never forget.

LILIAN

May I speak to you?

NATHAN

She took me by the hand, led me out on the terrace. Weaving through the crowd, I thought: all these years, and I've never had a real conversation with Arthur's wife. How is that? We're alone, looking down on Central Park. I start spouting price theory—

LILIAN

(Quietly.) Please stop. Please don't talk anymore.

(Pause.)

NATHAN

She puts her fingers on my mouth, holds them there, then glides back into the room. I watch her go, and my hands start to tremble. Because I realize, I want to do something terribly wrong.

LILIAN

I took my children to museums—I brought them here—because I wanted them to understand, so badly, that you must always be learning new things. This is the second of my golden rules.

"Seek out!" I would say. "Upend your expectations!"

"People are dangerous and not to be trusted." This is my third rule. Which I know is bracing, but then so is life. And if one does anything for one's children, one should prepare them for life. I wasn't all doom and gloom about it. I gently mixed it in: Mommy loves you, the Easter Bunny is coming, people are dangerous and not to be trusted. I never frightened my children. I was direct and I was honest, but I was never cruel. I worked so hard to keep us close. So they would tell me things. Let me see who they were becoming. Once—I treasure these memories; I hold them so dear—I took them to Mexico. When they were young. Just the three of us. Arthur was . . . absent. As always. June ate something local and improperly washed and spent the trip in her room, heaving, poor thing. Didn't see—didn't *do*—a thing. Gideon and I left her for only a few hours one afternoon, when she was sleeping, and went down to the beach. Just the two of us, hand in hand into the ocean. We swam out with fins and snorkels, peering down at the ocean floor, and cutting through the water we saw—and this is one of those things, somehow, you never forget. And why *this* and not something else? That's the mystery, isn't it? Why certain—and *only* certain—things are held on to, while the rest . . . swim away.

What we retain seems so random, without meaning. Yet we are defined by what we remember. Whether we know the reasons for that remembering or not.

(She smiles.)

And now I am right back at golden rule number one: totally lost, but going forward.

(Beat.)

It's only . . . how can you not wake up at night and ask yourself, what have I forgotten? What did I miss?

JUNE

I reread an old clipping from Paul this morning. He always loved to send me things. A postcard with thoughts about the rings of Saturn, an article about rural development in Nigeria—always with notes to me in the margins, in that precise handwriting of his, pointing out what he thought was important in case I might miss it.

The article was about those "Greek" statues, those precious few remaining marble figures of men and women that I grew up with, saw at the Met, other museums. The article explained that these beautiful objects—to me, almost sacred—are phony. *(Beat.)* I didn't know this.

The Greek originals *were* sacred. Not marble, but cast in solid bronze with silver teeth and copper lips. They were said to have appeared eerily human, their skin glowing in the Mediterranean sun. In the entire world, almost none survive. Melted down, destroyed, ages ago. The statues we think of as Greek original—"sacred"—are just fashionable trinkets. Marble imitations made hundreds of years later by the Romans. Pumped out as if by an assembly line and shipped all over the Empire as decoration. All pretending to be something they're not.

And this is the article's point: that these statues, like so much in this world, are not what they seem. That, in fact, they are duplicitous. Because once you see beyond the fact that they are beautiful and irreplaceable, nonetheless, you realize they're simply things that fool you into believing a lie.

Today, sitting here, I've been rereading everything Paul sent me during his six months in Africa. Every day I received a letter, a postcard, or a clipping, And then they stopped.

This article was the last thing Paul sent me. It's blank. I mean, no marginalia. He left the interpretation up to me.

NATHAN

Being in this room again makes me think of a *different* conference. Long after that night at the Doyle's, but still years ago. When I was doing my own work. Those conferences were always held in subdivided banquet rooms in a Best Western in St. Louis or Cincinnati. My presentations were always—"sparsely attended" is the nice way of putting it. Half a dozen people in the back, just a question or two at the end. This isn't uncommon. Every room on every floor had somebody reading something. This isn't a reflection on me. At least that's what I told myself. So when someone stays after and engages you, it's flattering. I'd finished my paper, everyone else had left, but this young fellow—graduate student, I'm thinking—he's stayed behind and starts peppering me with questions. I'd been talking on Bayesian Updating. The ripple effect that's caused by the introduction of new information. I'm elaborating on one of the more obtuse points. He's nodding. All the while I'm thinking, he looks like someone I know. He interrupts.

"Of course, things can get sticky when expectations are upended."

"How so?"

I can't place him. Driving me crazy.

He says, "Well, that's the danger of learning new things. If you keep digging, one day you'll discover that something you know in your bones, that defines who you are, is a lie."

A hotel full of economists, and I get stuck talking to Philosophy Boy.

"Well, thanks for sharing. I've got to—"

"Just one more question," he says.

I'm trying to get out the *door*, you understand. Networking, mingling—that's why I'm *here*.

"How long have you been fucking my mother?"

(Silence.)

I hadn't recognized him. Gid— *(Stops himself.)* Only Lilian called him that . . . Paul. I barely *knew* the boy, but he'd always dressed so . . . "pristine" is the word for it. Here . . . he was a different person. Ripped jeans. Torn sweater. Scruffy beard. His eyes . . . like he hadn't slept in days.

We're alone. He's staring at me. I can hear throat-clearing from someone's presentation in the room next door. And what do you do? What could I have said—*changed things*—at that moment.

(As if to him.) "It's not like that. . . . I would cut off my hands for her. . . . I'm so sorry."

. . . I say this in my mind. When I open my mouth . . . he's already gone.

LILIAN

(As if to him.) Would you teach me?

NATHAN

Solitaire.

LILIAN

I've never played.

NATHAN

That's how it started.

LILIAN

I'm not good with cards.

NATHAN

After that evening on the terrace, I swore to myself: just being near her, that will be enough. But one night, we were at dinner. Arthur at one end of their long table, me seated next to her at the other.

LILIAN

Please.

NATHAN

Life gives you what you want in strange ways. One moment you're dealing from a brand new deck, and then you're naked. And you have . . . everything.

There are things that happen to you, that define who you are, that should be *seared* into your memory. But when I try to recall them, when I need them *most* . . . they slip away. That first time Lilian and I . . . I don't remember a thing. Not one Goddamn thing. My life has become defined by what I *can't* remember. The things I *do* hold on to seem . . . like threads from the wrong pattern.

Here, now, what keeps coming to me—From when she first started flying us here. When we could finally spend days, instead of hours. It's night. I'm lying in that carved wooden bed. The moonlight, shimmering on the silk sheets. Watching her. She's naked, standing on that balcony with her back to me. She takes a draw on a cigarette, smoke rising up into the dark Roman night . . . The dark Roman night. There's a phrase she would have loved.

LILIAN

I don't do this.

NATHAN

She slips under the sheets, climbs on top of me.

LILIAN

This isn't me.

NATHAN

The same sentence, every time. And after a while—once, twice, a half dozen times, okay. But year after year after year—you have to say, "Yeah, this is me. I do this. I do this on a regular basis. And, by God, *I . . . get . . . something . . . from . . . this.*" *(Pause.)* What kind of a woman, sixty years on, has never been alone enough to learn solitaire? *(Pause.)* I still don't know what that means.

JUNE

Every step I've taken today, it's as if I can feel Paul getting closer to me. Everywhere I look, I see him. And Lily. All those times—God! It was so magical coming here, just the three of us. The cobbled streets, the history; seeing *everything*.

LILIAN

(As if to a child, sharply.) What did you say to him?

JUNE

But then, so often—out of the blue—Paul would recede.

LILIAN

Young lady, I am speaking to you.

JUNE

His eyes focused straight ahead.

LILIAN

What did you do to upset your brother?

JUNE

The outside world, falling away.

LILIAN

Why won't he open his door?

JUNE

I accepted this. I *knew* what he needed. But Lily—

LILIAN

Why do you always do this!

JUNE

I would get her to take me out alone, but when we came back—

LILIAN

June!

JUNE

She would thunder on his door—demanding, pushing—till he—

LILIAN

ANSWER ME!

JUNE

(Beat.) . . . Every night, after the fighting . . . Lily's tears and Paul's silence . . . I'd lead her out on that balcony and ask her to comb my hair. We'd be alone, and I'd say, *(As if to her.)* "Where are we going next, Mother."

LILIAN

(Beat. Then quietly . . .) Madagascar.

JUNE

(To us.) She'd lean down, whisper in my ear:

LILIAN

Madagascar. Soon.

JUNE

And everything was washed away. This thrill when she'd say it. Like electricity passing through me. The word would hang there, without a picture attached to it. Unencumbered by any sense of place or history. Out there . . . *(Points over our heads.)* waiting for us. Can you imagine how disappointed I was when I found it on a map? I was so young, I'd just been looking for "Africa," to know what *that* was. Because every time father left us . . .

LILIAN

He's in Africa.

JUNE

Is all she would say. She told Paul and me that Madagascar was a land *she'd* discovered. That it was just for the three of us. One day she'd take us, to where we wouldn't be lonely and there wouldn't be fighting. Where no one could come between us. Not even ourselves.

LILIAN

. . . I'm sorry. I'm so sorry, dear.

JUNE

I would sit between her legs as she whispered my name. Telling me what it meant.

LILIAN

June.

JUNE

Sunlight and evening breezes.

LILIAN

June.

JUNE

Bringer of showers, riser of lilies.

LILIAN & JUNE

(Together.)
June.

JUNE

And I knew she loved me, too.

LILIAN

Being in this room again, waiting for Gideon, I find it hard not to be anxious. Terrifying is how I find waiting for a plane's arrival.

This morning, here, counting the minutes until Gideon . . . You can imagine. But . . . the mystery is that whenever *I* fly . . . I feel released. Lifting into the air, piercing the clouds, I feel—somehow—free. To simply invent my answers.

MAN

(Chuckling.) Well, it's gonna be a long one!

LILIAN

I know it's unforgivable, but—God!—the relief!

WOMAN

(Cheerily.) Hope we get a movie!

LILIAN

To have protection, as I sit there . . .

MAN

So where'ya from?

LILIAN

Bombarded by question after question . . .

WOMAN

So where're ya going?

LILIAN

All leading to the dreaded . . .

MAN & WOMAN

(Together.)

So whada *you* do?

LILIAN

(As if speaking to her seatmates.) I'm an orthopedic surgeon.

MAN & WOMAN

(Together.)

Really!

LILIAN

Index fingers. They're my specialty.

WOMAN

I see!

LILIAN

On my way to a conference.

MAN

Where?

LILIAN

Madagascar.

MAN & WOMAN

(Together.)

Really!

LILIAN

Have you been?

MAN & WOMAN

(Together.)

Us? *(The couple laugh uproariously.)*

LILIAN

You'd be *amazed* at the number of surgical conferences in Madagascar.

MAN & WOMAN

(Together.)

(Fascinated.) I see!

LILIAN

(Back to us.) It's astounding what people will believe if you dress respectably. I do this for hours. And for a while, I am someone dif-

ferent. Someone who has an answer to the *real* question. The one beneath "What do *you* do." The question of:

"Who *are* you? No, no. Who are you *really*?"

(Pause. She smiles.)

I haven't the slightest idea. Daily, I catch myself in the mirror and I think, who is that, and why hasn't she had surgery? I am a mystery, even to myself. But if I could have my wish, high in the air, detached from the earth, when I am asked by some woman next to me—if I could be *honest*.

WOMAN

(Quietly.) Who are you?

LILIAN

Who do you want me to be?

WOMAN

My mother. My dead mother.

LILIAN

Then that's who I am. Come, let me cradle you in my arms. Let me kiss it and make it better. *(To us.)* And I would.

NATHAN

Arthur was fine when Lilian and I started, you understand. Healthy. Still in remission. "Nothing but clear skies ahead," he told me. Had it licked, he told me. But then she came to me, again and again, and slowly, over time, he . . . I'm not in a field that puts a lot of stock in coincidences.

I would sit at that long table of his with his children and his wife, who I could still taste, and he has tubes in his nose and people have to cut his meat. He's still laughing, holding court, everyone's clinking their silver, and the food in my mouth tastes like ashes. And I don't care. After dinner, a little brandy, a cigar, while I bite my tongue so I don't say:

"Yes, I'm fucking your wife, I'm slitting your throat, and *I . . . can't . . . stop.*"

At the funeral there wasn't a cloud in the sky. A roof of blue over our heads. We all looked out of place in our black suits and dresses. Like we were there for the wrong occasion.

LILIAN

(As if to other mourners.) Thank you so much for coming.

NATHAN

We didn't talk. Lilian didn't even look at me.

LILIAN

Your words were so comforting.

NATHAN

How could she look at me?

JUNE

(As if to the same group.) Yes, I'm sure my father would have.

NATHAN

I watched them, the remaining Doyles. Paul sat there, his mother on one side, his sister on the other. And between Lilian and June, you could feel this . . . their *need* for the boy. Crackling in the air. The two of them, sitting ramrod straight, their hair perfect. Like a couple of Greek goddesses, I thought. Vying for the same thing.

LILIAN

(Simultaneously.)

Thank you.

JUNE

(Simultaneously.)

No, I'm sure.

NATHAN

All through the service, my stomach in knots. Waiting for Paul to stand up, point at me, call down thunderbolts . . . Not a word. All day, Lilian and June moved about, greeting, comforting. All day, Paul sat there, still as a statue. Dressed the same way he'd been weeks ago when he confronted me at—Like some sort of punishment. When I was the one who—

JUNE

Nathan. May I speak to you?

[45]

NATHAN

(As if to her.) . . . I'm . . . June, I'm so—

JUNE

(Quietly.) No one else knows, Nathan. Be good to my mother. You're all she has left.

LILIAN

(To the assembled.) I couldn't agree more.

JUNE

Go forward. Don't look back.

LILIAN

Thank you. You've been so kind.

JUNE

Never look back.

NATHAN

(Beat. Then, to us . . .) Off to the side, Paul—she didn't notice—was watching her. Like he was . . . reading her.

June turns, then glides away. And I think:

How did she know? Lilian swore me to— I kept my word. No one was ever to— Here, now, I keep asking myself. *How . . . did . . . she . . . know?* That was the moment. Right then, I should have—

Goddamn it! It's what you *don't* do that tears everything down!

JUNE

There were so few times when there was peace between the three of us. I work very hard to hold onto those memories. Once—this is my earliest *real* memory, in which every detail is perfect—Lily took us to Mexico. My father was working. As always. Each morning, she'd take us down from our hotel room, with our snorkels and flippers. The water was so green it was like jade. She'd watch as Paul and I floated on the surface, looking down through our masks at the bottom covered in a forest of coral.

LILIAN

If you touch them, your fingers will burn.

JUNE

We kept diving down, closer and closer. Each time, tiny purple and orange fish shooting out of the anemones.

LILIAN

(*Calling cheerily from far away.*) Be careful!

JUNE

On the last day I asked Paul to plead with her, and she finally let us swim out away from the shore.

LILIAN

Stay close to your brother!

JUNE

The water was freezing! Our teeth chattered the whole time, but it was so exciting. The fish and the coral, a rainbow beneath us.

LILIAN

(Growing worried.) . . . That's far enough, dears!

JUNE

We kept going and going, trying to—

LILIAN

June, you're taking your brother too far!

JUNE

And then we saw it. This fish. Fluorescent black. Radiating light. We were so small then, it seemed as big as both of us. Swimming between our legs. Glowing, like something from another world. Paul was drawn to it. He reached for it, straining, trying to—

LILIAN

Come back, June!

JUNE

I yanked him back. Because what if its skin was poisoned? What if it turned on him and—

LILIAN

PLEASE!

JUNE

I still see it, sometimes. Cutting through the water, swimming ahead. It has a voice. It whispers and gurgles, but I can't—not with all the water between us. I churn my arms and legs, trying to get nearer, because I know it's holding secrets underneath the waves, but I don't know what it wants, and I wake up and I remember that he's still missing. That my brother is missing. For five years. My mother was waiting for him, here, in this room. But he never got off the plane.

Paul never got off the plane.

(Lights fade to black.)

ACT TWO

Sherri Parker Lee as June and Mary Beth Peil as Lilian in the Off-Broadway Summer Play Festival production of *Madagascar*. Photo by Carol Rosegg.

Act Two

Lights reveal the three of them, on stage as before. Behind them the projected image of the Spanish Steps, but darker now; twilight.

JUNE *steps toward us.*

JUNE

When someone disappears, the longer it takes for your search to begin, statistically, the odds are less and less in your favor. If the scent is already cold when you start . . . there are too many cases for yours to have any urgency. (*Beat.*) I didn't know this.

When the police get involved, if they find no immediate evidence of wrongdoing, they quickly lose interest. Those who can't be found *chose* to vanish, they tell you. Nine times out of ten, they tell you.

When you don't accept this, you hire private detectives. And when they also find no definitive answer, and reach the same conclusion . . . that the vanishing must have been planned . . . you reject this. You get involved personally.

(LILIAN *and* NATHAN *step down toward us as one.*)

FEMALE RELIEF WORKER

(*A British accent.*) I don't know what to say, Miss Doyle.

JUNE

I flew halfway around the world.

MALE RELIEF WORKER

(A French accent.) He told us he was leaving for the airport.

JUNE

To the precise location he'd vanished from.

FEMALE RELIEF WORKER

We all saw him take his bag and walk away.

JUNE

His fellow aid workers were exactly how Paul had described them in his letters.

MALE RELIEF WORKER

We expected him back. Books, clothes—everything is still here.

JUNE

Working with them, he felt part of something. A purpose.

FEMALE RELIEF WORKER

He said he needed some time away.

JUNE

"Helping people here," he wrote me, "nothing will ever come close to this."

MALE RELIEF WORKER

(With difficulty.) You see, Paul was not . . . He did not really fit in here.

JUNE

They didn't know if they should tell me at first. Kept glancing at each other, not wanting to offend.

MALE RELIEF WORKER

It's just . . . I do not think he was cut out for this.

JUNE

At first he plunged in, they told me. Like all of them. But then . . .

FEMALE RELIEF WORKER

(Trying to soothe.) It's very difficult work.

JUNE

Day after day, the heat, then the dysentery . . .

MALE RELIEF WORKER

Maybe because of his background.

JUNE

. . . the *struggle* to just . . .

FEMALE RELIEF WORKER

(With a shrug.) We are who we are.

JUNE

. . . making him distant . . .

FEMALE RELIEF WORKER

We're so sorry.

JUNE

. . . angry . . .

FEMALE RELIEF WORKER

He was a good man.

JUNE

(Exploding, as if at the woman.) You did not *know* him! YOU KNEW NOTHING ABOUT HIM!

(Pause. She collects herself. Then back to us.)

I left Africa and flew back to New York with Paul's address book. So many friends he'd been writing. So many names I didn't even know. I contacted everyone, asked the exact same questions:

"Have you seen, when did you *last* see, when did you last *hear* from, do you have—*please* . . . anything."

They all told me the same thing. He'd written them regularly, until—just before he left for his plane—he stopped. All of us. The exact same time.

LILIAN

(As if on the phone.) Where is he? Did you make Gideon miss his flight?

JUNE

But when they showed me his letters and postcards to *them* . . . they read like they'd been written by a stranger.

LILIAN

Put him on the phone. You can't horde him, June.

JUNE

Card after letter—his sense of failure. That he'd flown halfway around the world, to strip his life bare, cut everything away.

LILIAN

Of *course* he's there. He wrote me at the lake house that he would visit you in New York for a week, then meet me here in Rome.

JUNE

"But you can't escape who you are," he wrote. "No matter how much you try."

LILIAN

I've flown in from Geneva!

JUNE

"Now, where will I go?" he wrote.

LILIAN

(Growing frightened.) . . . I don't understand.

JUNE

"What will I do?"

LILIAN

I did what he asked!

JUNE

"How will I be released?"

LILIAN

June! *(Beat.)* WHERE IS HE!?!

NATHAN

When information is buried, it's human nature to want to dig it up, pull it up by the roots, and give it a shake.

Here—now—I can't stop thinking about Paul. About his absence. Its ramifications. I never *knew* him. The only real conversation we ever had was our little get-to-know-you at the Best Western. All those years ago. But here, today . . . this image keeps coming to me. Those parties at the House of Doyle. When I'd come in, during the kisses and hellos and can-I-take-your-coat, there he'd be. Standing in the middle of his parents' living room, mouth running, just *burning* with what he had to say. And, really, is there anything worse in this world than listening to a man under thirty with something to say?

But you couldn't *not* look at him. Impeccably dressed, offensively thick head of black hair. And his hands! Every time, I'd think, "God, those are beautiful hands." Which I found strange because men's digits are not a particular fetish of mine. But his were. Beautiful. Just like his father: the same poise, charisma. God, he worshipped Arthur! You could *see* Paul trying to copy his father's mannerisms. The way he'd rock back on his heels, the distracted air . . . but there was a difference. With Paul, there was this . . . intensity. Almost feverish. His movements, expressions—like there was too much of . . . *something* . . . coursing through him. Couldn't be contained.

At the parties, he'd stand there, torrent of words coming out of his mouth, eyes blazing. And those hands, they'd be gesticulating like crazy. As if they had a life of their own. From across the room, watching his fingers go up and down, like something in code. Faster and faster. I can see them trembling, like the bones inside are straining against his skin, trying to rip out, trying to *free* themselves. And every time—this is *before,* you understand. When he didn't know that his mother and I were—when everything should have been *fine*—I stood there and thought:

"What's wrong with you, son? What are you running from?"

LILIAN

After these six months of silence, you can imagine Gideon's invitation to meet here was quite unexpected. But if you are honest, there comes a point where you must acknowledge that even the people closest to you, even your children, are strangers. And that there will always be secrets between you.

Waiting for Gideon in this room, full of so many memories . . . The difference in my relationship with my two children comes sharply into focus.

My daughter is uninterested in any of this. She finds it—I'm not sure—tedious, perhaps? Uninspiring? June lives in New York and works in—something to do with number crunching.

JUNE

(*As if to her, correcting, once again.*) Corporate finance.

LILIAN

She tells me.

JUNE

I make the engine go.

LILIAN

Where to? I want to ask, but that wouldn't be . . . well-received.

I love my daughter. After all, I birthed her and Gideon and raised them almost single-handedly in the era before men became sensitive and maternal and what a nightmare that's been. But she does not care for me. It would be best in her eyes if I were gone. Not dead, but . . . absent. To raise a child and, at the end, to find her distant. To realize that there is a gulf between you, no bridge in sight. How I regret that.

But when June was young, I tried so hard to light that spark. When we were here—just the three of us—Gideon would so often ask to stay in the room. To write letters and postcards home to everyone about what he'd seen, done. His excitement! The blaze in his eyes! Goose bumps. Every time. I would seize the opportunity, take her to the Forum, climb the Palatine— *(As if pointing out the sights to her.)* There, June. What do you see?

JUNE

(As a girl, tentatively.) The Curia.

LILIAN

Yes! And there?

JUNE

. . . Arch of Septimus Severus.

LILIAN

Good! And that, there? *(No response.)* You *know* it, June. The house where all the good little girls go. Say it with me, dear. The . . .

LILIAN & JUNE

(Together.) House of the Vestal Virgins.

LILIAN

Look at you! Look at what you know! Aren't you a lucky girl? *(Back to us.)* But she was only humoring me. Such a shrewd child.

With each expedition, she was only marking time until she could return here to our room and they could be reunited. Siblings should be apart. At least at times. This is healthy. Natural. But June . . . she wilted without him. When I would take her, it was like I was tearing food from her mouth. Gideon—he was *always* stronger, so much more sure of himself—she worshipped him. Like when you are madly in love for the first time and your skin . . . how it aches for his touch. How nothing else matters, and all you want is to be ravished. And even then you know that nothing else will ever come close to this. And you must hold on to this burning as long as you can.

NATHAN

I never told Lilian any of this. The parties, the hands, the Best Western. None of it. Not even that June knew about us. I'd planned to—always—but . . . after my confrontation with Paul, I wanted to give him space. Time. It was up to *him* to talk to her first about—to *choose* the moment he . . .

I owed him that. But he never said a word.

Then Arthur died. After the funeral, I assumed Lilian's guilt would be too much for her. So I waited for the phone call. Her, ending us. I'll tell her then, I told myself. But she came back. Climbing on top of me, needing me. Me, afraid to even breathe. Afraid if she knew what I'd kept from her, I'd lose her forever.

Then, out of the blue, when the boy left—No, Goddamn it! He abandoned them! Packed up and shipped out, his father not even cold in the ground!

LILIAN

What did I do?

NATHAN

Tell her *then*?

LILIAN

What drove him away?

NATHAN

Everything I'd kept from her? That if she'd *known*, things could have been—

LILIAN

(As if to Nathan, a trembling whisper.) I don't know what I did.

NATHAN

I tried everything I could to ease her—

LILIAN

What have I forgotten?

NATHAN

But I couldn't find the, the right *words* to—

LILIAN

What did I miss?

NATHAN

Couldn't *articulate* what she needed me to—

LILIAN

Tell me! *Please*! What did I miss?

NATHAN

And June . . . how could I have told *her* about Paul? I couldn't even *begin* to find the . . . I would see her sitting alone, staring out the windows. I don't have any siblings so I don't *know*, but to have a twin must . . . She and Paul were fraternal but, somehow, mirror images of each other. Like they were one and the same. The strength that must come from that kind of connection. To have that, and then to have that severed . . . I would think that would feel like being killed.

JUNE

Paul never wrote me about coming to see me in New York. And that afterward, he was meeting Lily here. When she called me from this room . . .

I had no idea that he wrote and told her this. From the moment he left for Africa, he *never* wrote her. Six months, not a word. Lily and I, under the same roof. Each day, I'd send him a letter, receive a postcard. Each one a slap. A finger in her wound. She never acknowledged that something had changed between them. Her face a mask, hard, unmoving. Making me afraid to ask her what—I should have asked *him*. Pleaded her case. I don't know why I didn't. But then I don't know why he uprooted his life and went there in the first place. The only explanation he ever gave . . .

This was right after our father's funeral. When Lily spent days and days upstairs in their room. When Paul would never go up and see her, no matter how many times I asked. We were in the living room, it was raining—

"Madagascar."

He says this. Out of the blue. We were talking about . . . I can't remember.

"I'm going to Madagascar."

At first I don't under . . . I realize what he means. To *go* there. All the years we . . . this wasn't part of our—

"Tomorrow."

Something in his eyes. A shift.

"I thought you'd like to know."

He's staring at me. I can't think straight. Can't find the right words.

(To him.) " . . . Why?"

"You haven't been paying attention."

He looks at me, unblinking.

"You know why."

What did he mean by that? I should have understood. I should have *known*. He wouldn't have gone. None of this would have happened. That was the moment. We're standing by the windows, the rain coming down. And all I say is:

(To him.) " . . . But . . . why?"

He looks off to one side. Runs his hands through his hair.

"Because people can't be trusted."

LILIAN

When June grew older, she would *always* turn to Gideon. In her room, behind closed doors, I would hear them giggling. Whispering. And they would come down to dinner, and there would be these little winks. A raised eyebrow, a phrase between mouthfuls I couldn't understand. Like a code only they shared. Even when she should have been out with girls her own age chasing boys, gossiping on the phone, she would lure him into her room and lock the door . . . and it would be quiet for the longest time.

NATHAN

After Paul's disappearance, Lilian turned to me like never before. When we were alone. But in public, she made us keep on like we always had. And after a while, to still find yourself something that has to be hidden. At parties, still having to strain for a look, fight for a moment alone. To be something that can't be looked in the face without shame. After a while, that starts to eat at you.

LILIAN

(As if answering the phone.) Yes, this is Lilian Doyle.

NATHAN

Starts to make you angry.

LILIAN

Yes, I'll accept the charges.

NATHAN

Till all you want to do is take the pattern your life is trapped in and smash it like a plate.

LILIAN

(Eagerly.) June! Hello!

NATHAN

But when June finally called home—*two years* she looked for Paul. All over the world.

LILIAN

Where are you? What have you—tell me! Do you—

NATHAN

Gave up her job. Her life.

LILIAN

Do you . . . *(Silence. Then very calmly . . .)* I see.

NATHAN

When she told Lilian Paul *had* to be dead. That all evidence— There was nothing more she could—

LILIAN

I see.

NATHAN

Lilian accepted this. She moved on.

LILIAN

Well. Thank you.

NATHAN

She never spoke of him again, and she moved on.

LILIAN

I'm sure you did your best.

NATHAN

She hung up the phone, we lay in bed, and she told me she was finally going to tell June—the *world* about—there was nothing in the way anymore. We could move on.

(Pause.)

We should have had the chance to move on.

JUNE

What did Paul mean by that? Today, going back over everything he wrote me . . . I see all sorts of clues. But I can't . . . The tone of his letters, the content. So much more distant than I remember. Angry. As if I'd—

What did I do? How did I fail him?

I looked for Paul, every moment of every day for two years, until I had to stop. Salvage my own life. Start looking at my feet. One step in front of another. But after I accepted he was gone, even after all the years I've spent here . . . How did he die? An accident, murdered, or did he kill himself. Did he swallow pills or use a weapon. Did he walk up into the rain forest that morning and just keep going. Because, if we're honest, we have to acknowledge that people kill themselves all the time. (*Beat.*) My mother, for example. Well, that's *my* assumption. Officially, there was no proof. Officially, it was an accident. But to have happened so soon after I finally called and told her Paul *had* to be . . . Lily was too far from the shore. It was night. It's very foolish to swim in a lake at night. The water that time of year, that high in the mountains, would numb your skin. Ice your veins. Swimming through that, after a while your limbs would feel like stone. She swam out, away from the shore, and then she slipped under.

LILIAN

When I would try to speak to Gideon about June—about her . . . attachment to him . . . he would slip away. Without fail, leaving me a note, where he knew I'd find it. An epigram or a riddle to be deciphered, neatly written on a postcard. This is how Gideon has *always* preferred to communicate. Especially about the difficult things.

"Distance, Mother, helps make sense of things."

I still write, of course, but he no longer replies. Not since he went to Africa. He sent *one* thing, just after he arrived. I reread the clipping over and over again this morning on the flight here. The headline:

"Girls' Boarding School Attacked by Local Men."

For once there were no markings in the margins. The attack took place—I can't remember. Somewhere in Africa. It was night. Men came through windows, smashing glass, breaking down doors. The teachers fled. After all, these girls weren't *their* children. The girls were fifteen. Younger. In the picture in the article, their black skin—and I know it's incorrect to speak like this—is so beautiful. The color of eggplant, or a deep bruise. They wore uniforms: white blouses, patent-leather shoes. They were raped. Almost all of them. In the darkness, they were dragged out into the fields. Where some of them were killed. Where they were found with knife wounds in their . . . I put the article down. Some things cannot be looked at. You must simply go forward. And this is why he sent it. To point out, again, my great failing. Because I am like most people: fifteen-year-old girls on the other side of the world are raped and murdered, and I do not care. Of course, I'm horrified. "Oh, those poor children! Did you see the photos? Someone should *do* something! Someone should try!" But that someone is never me. My life goes on as if it never happened. And my *in*action ensures that things like this—and worse—will go on, everywhere, every day. It is what we *don't* do that we deserve to be punished for. And this failing in me, how it disgusts him. That morning, our last terrible morning, he made that so very clear.

NATHAN

My work has been a great comfort these last few years. To be able to immerse myself in . . . I've been grateful for that. And I believed—foolishly, of course; I see that now—that I was . . . "free" is the best word for it.

(He takes a moment to look around the room.)

When they first let me in here this morning . . . this ornate room had been stripped of— Almost unrecognizable.

EMBASSY WOMAN

(On a telephone, a bad connection.) Buon giorno? Mr. Sanders?

NATHAN

White walls. Naked lightbulb.

EMBASSY WOMAN

Can you hear me?

NATHAN

Like a prison cell.

EMBASSY WOMAN

Mr. Sanders, I'm calling about June Doyle.

NATHAN

Someone from the embassy here had gotten involved. Hotel manager must have contacted them.

EMBASSY WOMAN

I'm so sorry.

NATHAN

June had been dead for a few days before they found her and called me. No one had reported her missing. No one seemed to know her. She was very thorough. They told me she used the exact right mixture of pills. She was in her bed in a white linen nightgown. Hair, beautifully combed, the manager told me. She stressed that. June's fingers were locked together *(demonstrates)*, holding a note against her chest. All it said—*she* wrote it; apparently there's no question about that—

"Please call Nathan Sanders. Tell him, I looked back."

LILIAN

"I'm leaving," Gideon says.

We're home. I'm alone at the table, reading. He's at the top of the stairs, looking down on me.

"Where to?" I ask, expecting he's off on one of those endless walks he's started taking. Ever since Arthur's death. Every day, longer and longer.

"I won't be back," he says.

Something finite in his tone. Like he's already gone.

"I'm tired of all this."

Again, I bite my tongue. The way he's started to dress: his pants, stained and wrinkled. Every day, the same faded blue shirt.

"My car's waiting."

How unshaven, thin he's— Ever since his father's— What does this mean? What am I missing?

(As if to him.) "But . . . where are you going, dear?"

"Madagascar."

" . . . Why?"

He smiles so cruelly as he answers this.

"Because so much of what I believe in is a lie."

There in our dining room, I block his way. I will not let him move until he explains. Everything he owns, sold or given away, he says. A monk. That's—yes, what he looked like, standing in the morning sunlight. On a penniless pilgrimage, turning his back on everything. Gifts are not to be squandered. To be given everything and to throw it away is unforgivable. A woman who would let that happen is not a mother. And so it all comes out, and things are said, in the heat of it, that you both wish you could—and finally he says—inches from me, word for word:

"You are selfish. You are grotesque. God, how I pity you."

What do you say to that? To look at your son, standing across from you, planning to throw away his life, and hear the disgust dripping in his voice, while your brain can only scream: I was cut open for you. I was peeled and then sewn back so you could have everything. In that moment, you have to make a choice. I spit in his face. *(Pause.)* I spit in my son's face. *(Pause.)* We have not spoken since.

JUNE

Lily's funeral, back home in New York, was overflowing. Afterward, at the apartment, everyone awkwardly held little plates of food as we wove back and forth from the canapés to the punch bowl. I don't know who had the idea for a pink champagne punch bowl, but she would have liked that.

FUNERAL GUEST

My dear, I don't know *what* to say.

JUNE

I stood in the corner trying to fend off conversation.

FUNERAL GUEST

I'm *so* sorry.

JUNE

Because you get so tired of hearing that.

FUNERAL GUEST

I'm *so*—

JUNE

The emptiness of it makes you want to punch things.

NATHAN

June.

JUNE

He was standing in front of me, both hands clutching a glass.

NATHAN

May I speak to you.

JUNE

My mother's lover. Alone. *(As if to Nathan.)* How nice to see you, Nathan. Thank you for coming. *(To us.)* How many years had he waited for her?

NATHAN

If we could . . . Just for a moment.

JUNE

Looking at him, I couldn't remember when I first learned . . . As a girl, what I must have stumbled on.

NATHAN

Out on the terrace.

JUNE

I never told her, never told anyone. Not even Paul.

NATHAN

I need to tell you something.

JUNE

I wanted her to be happy. For this to be *our* secret. She could trust me.

NATHAN

Please.

JUNE

God! It was such a relief to get some privacy and fresh air! Look down on Central Park and escape from . . . He started to cry.

The moment we were alone. Heaving like a wounded animal. He grabbed my hands:

NATHAN

If there's anything I can ever do for you.

JUNE

The fervency in his voice.

NATHAN

Anything. Remember that.

JUNE

Your parents meant so much to me, he said. I loved them, he said. Please forgive me, he said. I put my hand on his face, and there was this slight shock of static electricity. Both of us flinching. And right then, I wanted him to kiss me. Pin my wrists, pry me open, and penetrate me. Till I burned.

There are some things we're not allowed to forget. No matter how much we try. A hundred people were inside sipping punch, my mother was in the *ground* . . . Today, I can't stop thinking about this moment. Standing out there, aching for him, as he said her name and had to turn away.

NATHAN

I don't do this.

JUNE

Covering his eyes.

NATHAN

This isn't me.

JUNE

Shamed by his tears. His hands, trembling.

NATHAN

Why would June choose me? She made me the . . . I am now the inheritor of their estate. The House of Doyle. Me. I was sitting at my desk, editing a speech I give in two days, the phone rings, and—I have spent *years* working toward this. *I . . . should . . . not . . . be . . . here.* But here I am, standing in the room—this room—where Lilian and I used to . . .

(Beat.) This is the same room. *(Beat.)* I don't know what that means.

JUNE

After Lily was gone . . . after my father, and my brother, and then my mother . . . I thought I had a choice: follow the pattern set down by the rest of my family, or break it. Go forward, or look back. I cut my losses and moved here. One step in front of another. One day, then the next. For years. Life teaches you who you are in the most unexpected ways.

This morning, with my paper and coffee, there was a letter—hopefully the last paperwork dealing with the estate—and a postcard. Which in itself is strange, because who would know to find me here. It's the first real mail I've received in . . . I can't remember how long. The card was glossy, brand new. The picture on the front is a beach resort, hot and crowded. Sand and ocean and high-rise hotels, I'm sure just full of people from Morristown, New Jersey. I flipped it over. On the back are my name and address, precisely written. The note is three words:

"I'm . . . still . . . here."

LILIAN

And now, in this room again, clock ticking, all I can think is:

"What will I say?"

Such a simple and terrifying question. My son—my darling boy—will be here any moment. His plane is landing, even as I speak. I have waited for this for so long. But when he stands in front of me, what will I say? How will we be able to go forward? I cannot bear losing him again. I will not live through that again.

NATHAN

When they let me in here this morning, June's things had been left untouched. By the window . . . the strangest thing. A bed, a nightstand, a table and one chair. The whole room, that's it. And on the nightstand, a coffee cup, a newspaper, and a postcard.

The picture is of a beach resort. Some warm-weather tourist spot. Could be anywhere in the world. On the back, the postmark is smudged. The card has been . . . clawed at. Touched so many times, you can make out the oil stains from a set of fingers. The corners are ragged and torn. And the message . . . Like someone's used their fingernails to scratch it out. Scraped back and forth, over and over, till you can't read a thing. Then left it on the nightstand. All by itself. Indecipherable.

JUNE

All day—coffee, tour, home—

What does this mean?

Sitting here, pouring over all his cards, letters—

What does he want from me?

To say to me?

Do to me?

He could be arriving—here, any moment—walk through that door, and what do I *do*? How do I *see* him . . . Knowing he planned all this. Tore everything down.

Some things cannot be looked at. Some things cannot be faced.

(She holds up a postcard.)

This is not my life.

NATHAN

Tunnel vision: that's the mark of a second-rate economist. Something happens, you try to decipher. Understand how it connects to a larger pattern. But you get trapped by the questions:

Who sent this? What does it mean?

You ask over and over, until you realize you've committed the fatal error: you've let the details of reality blind you to the truth.

"We untangle secrets and mysteries," Arthur said, "step by step." But he was wrong. They're not the same. A secret is an answer waiting to be revealed. But a mystery . . .

(He looks around the room.)

Is just that: a mystery.

LILIAN

When they were children, it was so simple. I cherish these memories, I hold them so dear. Once . . . Yes! What I was saying before! That time in Mexico . . . When Gideon and I swam out, cutting through the water, hand in hand, over fields of coral. A rainbow beneath us. Seared into my memory is the image of this great black fish. Swimming toward the two of us, somehow glowing with light. Gideon reached toward it, wanting to touch it, his fingers almost—I pulled him back . . . and it swam away.

But *afterward,* in the hotel, is what I treasure. We returned, both of us, our shoulders pink and blistering. The windows were open and a ceiling fan carried in the afternoon breeze. June lay sleeping in my bed, her hair splayed out like tentacles. Her tiny face, pressed against the sheets. I lay down, still wet from the ocean, with Gideon and June in my arms. Under the whirl of those fan blades, thinking of nothing. Emptying myself.

NATHAN

Yesterday, back in New York, when I got the call that brought me here, and this you'll find interesting . . . I was in a taxi, on my way to the airport. We were driving by the Met, and the idea just came to me. I asked the driver to make a quick stop, and to keep the meter running.

Even that early in the morning, the Met was already full. People milling about, wearing their audio guides. I didn't need one. Lilian had described it so clearly, so often, I felt like I'd stood in front of it before. Even for someone like me, it's impressive.

The panel is a good ten feet high, half as wide. A carving of three figures in profile. On the left is Demeter, the Greek goddess of agriculture and abundance. On the right, her daughter Persephone, queen of the underworld. A plaque on the wall tells you all this. The way they're carved—faces, clothes, expressions—they look exactly the same. As if they were the same person. Both of them extend their right hand toward a boy, naked, standing between them, his face turned upward. His right hand reaches out, too, but . . . she never told me this part . . . all of their fingers are missing, as if cut away. What they were giving, reaching for, it's impossible to tell. No one knows what they held, or what was supposed to happen next. Just another mystery.

LILIAN

But what has given me hope, what has allowed me to get through this day . . . Life gives you what you need so unexpectedly. Flying here this morning . . . the most extraordinary thing. We were high in the air, piercing the clouds . . .

FELLOW TRAVELER

And what do *you* do?

LILIAN

(She opens her mouth, ready to take on a new persona . . . Pause. Then . . .) I am a mother.

FELLOW TRAVELER

Really.

LILIAN

. . . I have two children.

FELLOW TRAVELER

How wonderful!

LILIAN

. . . Yes. Yes it is. *(To us.)* If who you are is what you have done . . . *They* are what I have done. How remarkable to realize that all you are truly defined by are those you bring into the world. Then leave behind. What will they do, I wonder. How much more wisdom than me will they glean? Now, here, I will find a way to bridge, and bring Gideon home.

FELLOW TRAVELER

Where are you headed?

LILIAN

Rome. (*Then to us.*) Isn't it wonderful how one word can hold so much?

(*The lights have dimmed and* LILIAN *and* NATHAN *are only shadow figures now. Behind them we see a projected image of the ocean, of dark, undulating waves.*)

JUNE

Paul and I made each other laugh. I remember giggling, holding hands. When we were alone, when we were children, we would slip away. To play *our* game. Our version, just for the two of us. A secret within a secret. We would go to my room and lock the door. We'd sit down and I'd say:

"Who am I?"

(As Paul, eagerly.) "You're a goddess!"

"Who am I?"

"You're, you're a vestal virgin!"

"Who am I?"

He'd hold out as long as he could. Build up the excitement.

"Who am I *really*?"

"You're mother."

Like electricity, just saying it out loud. I'd take his hand and we'd close our eyes.

(She does so.)

"Where are we going next, Mother?"

"Madagascar," I'd say.

"On a magic carpet?"

"Yes."

"Made of gossamer wings?"

"Yes."

"Tell me."

(June stands in a shaft of light. As she speaks, Lilian comes out of the darkness and drifts down to her.)

I'd say, just like her, "We'll fly over the ocean . . . "

(Lilian joins in, as if to her children.)

JUNE & LILIAN

(Together.)

"Going higher, piercing the clouds. And there it will be, shimmering."

LILIAN

(Continuing on her own.) Splayed out before us, full of vestal virgins, and beautiful children, and wonderful, wonderful things.

(June opens her eyes and smiles.)

JUNE

Goose bumps. Every time.

(The light fades to darkness.

End of play.)

About the Author

J.T. Rogers's *Madagascar* received the 2005 Pinter Review Prize for Drama and the American Theatre Critics Association's 2004 M. Elizabeth Osborne Award, and was a finalist for the ATCA's Steinberg New Play Award. *Madagascar* was recently produced Off Broadway as part of the SPF Summer Play Festival, and at the Adirondack Theatre Festival, the New Theatre in Miami, and the Salt Lake Acting Company. Rogers is the author of *White People* (L.A. Drama Critics Circle and Barrymore Award nominees for best play of the year), *Seeing the Elephant* (Kesselring Prize nominee for best new American play), and *Murmuring in a Dead Tongue,* which was presented last season in New York City by Epic Rep, where he is company member. His latest play, *The Overwhelming,* was presented in 2005 at the inaugural PlayPenn festival of new works in Philadelphia. His plays have been produced in New York City at The Next Stage, where he is a founding member, and regionally at the Williamstown Theatre Festival, Philadelphia Theatre Co., the New Theatre, New Actors Union Theatre (Moscow), the Road Theatre (L.A.), and many times at the Salt Lake Acting Co., where he was a 2004-2005 NEA/TCG playwright-in-residence. Rogers has been an artist in residence at the Eugene O'Neill Theater Center and the Edward Albee Foundation, and was the recipient of a 2004 playwriting fellowship from the New York Foundation for the Arts. He has been a guest artist at Truman State University in Missouri and has lectured at the North Carolina School of the Arts' and University of Utah's schools of drama and at the Claremont McKenna School of Economics. For three seasons he was on faculty at New York University as part of the Creative Arts Team, where he taught conflict resolution through drama in at-risk junior high schools in Brooklyn and the Bronx. Rogers is a graduate of the professional actor-training program at the North Carolina School of the Arts. He lives in Brooklyn.

About the Book

The title of *Madagascar* on cover and title page is set in Hadriano, a font designed by Frederic Goudy about 1918. He developed the type from three chiseled letters on an inscribed marble monument dating from the first century and bearing an inscription that included the word "Hadriano." The letterforms had caught Goudy's eye during a 1910 visit to the Louvre Museum in Paris, and he surreptitiously captured them as rubbings in his notebook for future study. Goudy's designs were adapted for digital release in 2005 by the P22 Type Foundry in its Lanston Type Company series. The emblem appearing with Hadriano type in section titles is adapted from the Greek marble relief projected as part of the stage set in *Madagascar*. The text of the book is set in Adobe Garamond Pro, based on a sixteenth century roman font of Claude Garamond, with a complementary italic type by Robert Granjon. The book was designed and typeset by Richard Mathews at the University of Tampa Press. It has been printed on acid-free Glatfelter Natures Natural recycled text papers and bound in Brillianta cloth from Ecological Fibers, Inc., in support of the Green Press Initiative, by Thomson-Shore of Dexter, Michigan.